ACTUALLY, CLAMS ARE MISERABLE

Also by Bryan Allain

31 Days to Finding Your Blogging Mojo

Community Wins

ACTUALLY, CLAMS ARE MISERABLE

Deconstructing 101 Ridiculous Clichés

Bryan Allain

Written by Bryan Allain | @bryanallain
Foreword by Bryan Allain | @bryanallain
Cover & all illustrations by Wes Molebash | @thewesmolebash
Edited by Andi Cumbo | @andilit
Completely ignored by Seth Meyers | @sethmeyers21

4 8 15 16 23 42
ISBN: 978-0-9883729-0-0

MENU OF CONTENTS

FOREWORD

Actually, Clams Are Miserable

I first met Bryan Allain sometime in the 1970s. He cried a lot more back then and didn't know how to wipe his own butt.

As the story goes, his parents were often afraid to go out of the house with him during those first few months for fear he would break into another one of his legendary colic episodes.

These days Bryan does a lot more laughing than crying. And frankly, a lot more of his own butt wiping as well.

I've known Bryan for 36 years now and I have to say few people enjoy making others laugh more than Bryan does. I know that's why he wrote this book. So please chuckle, snicker, smile, and laugh as the spirit moves.

You know, this foreword really isn't working out as well as I thought it would. I guess that's why people usually don't write their own forewords.

Good to know for the next book.

- Bryan Allain

Actually, Clams Are Miserable

BY THE NUMBERS

"We've got to give 110%."

Few things frustrate me more than clichés that fly in the face of logic. Clearly, no one can give more than 100% of themselves because it's all they have. Once you hit 100%, the only way to give more is to start giving away other people's energy and effort.

Come to think of it, maybe that's why I'm sitting on the couch right now. I thought it was because I was lazy, but it turns out your softball coach just got you a little too fired up for today's exhibition game and now my to-do list is paying for it. You stole some of MY effort so you could give 110%, you punk!

So go ahead, dive for that foul ball you had no chance of catching. I guess I'll just trim the shrubs some other time when they're not airing a Seinfeld marathon.

While you're in hustle mode, go make me a sandwich.

"Let's give it the old college try!"

Not sure what college you went to, but at my school, 'trying' meant getting out of bed before noon.

I can't think of a group of people who tried LESS than college students, unless you're talking about procrastinating on homework and putting off starting important projects, in which case, yes, a great effort was put forth. Heroic, even.

Maybe we should say, "Give it the old 'I'm in second grade and I care about my grades because I'm still under the delusion that they mean something' try"?

"I really did a number on it."

Are you making a statement, or is this a game? Am I supposed to guess what kind of number you did on it?

Was it an actual number? Twenty...two? It was twenty-two, wasn't it?

Wait – was it a theatrical number? Man, that could be anything from *Cats* to *Amadeus*. Can I have a hint? Was it *Newsies*? Blink twice if it was *Newsies*.

I don't think I like this game.

Here's a better idea: if we really want to communicate that we negatively made an impact on something, let's change it from, "I really did a number on it" to, "I really did a number two on it". A bit crass, I know, but it does help get the point across.

Unless, of course, you're talking about how quickly you ate your lunch. I don't want to hear about how you did a number two on that. That's kind of gross.

"You should count your blessings."

One, two, three, four...

What's the point of this? Is this supposed to make me feel better?

Five, six, seven, eight...

This doesn't seem to be working.

Nine, ten, eleven, twelve...

Can I think about my blessings instead of counting them? Or maybe if I could just talk about them with someone? That might help.

No? Fine.

Thirteen, fourteen, fifteen, sixteen...

"A penny for your thoughts?"

Oh wow! You cherish my opinion so much that you equate it with the honor and valor bestowed upon Abraham Lincoln, whose noble face adorns this zinc and copper circle.

Yes, I will speak to you with the same wisdom and power that our 16th president manifested in the face of a divided country.

Listen intently and know that I will do everything I can to live up to the exorbitant amount of money you've just given me in exchange for my thoughts on the matter.

I'm so glad that honest Abe gave his life to preserve freedom in this country so you could stand here centuries later and insult me and my family with that turd bomb of an offer.

You want my thoughts? I'm thinking you can take your penny and shove it in *the remainder of this page was redacted to preserve the honor of President Lincoln and the United States of America. Trust us, it got ugly quick.*

"We were piss poor."

It was probably the worst of my father's crazy ideas.

Looking back, I'm not sure what prompted his wacky hunch that someday urine would be accepted as a viable form of currency.

Had he been right, and had urine replaced the dollar, things would have been totally different for us. We would have been piss-rich.

Instead, we just had a basement full of old pee.

"Crime doesn't pay."

If it did, all these criminals would be able to find gainful employment instead of robbing banks and stealing people's identities to make a living.

Maybe if we find a way to legalize crime so the government can tax it, this world would be a safer place for all of us. Now that would be a political platform I could get behind! Heck, I might just run myself.

LEGALIZE CRIME, VOTE ALLAIN!

I'm Bryan Allain, and I approve this message.

"He's got the skills that pay the bills."

But really, with Automatic Bill Pay how much skill does it really take these days?

Ooh, he knows how to use a mouse and type in an 8-digit account number on a website!!!

In that case, my 8-year old has the skills to pay the bills, too.

"She's got a new lease on life."

Sucks for her.

I mean, it's great that things have turned around for her, but now she's got to make monthly payments, she's got to watch her mileage, and there's probably going to be a turn-in fee in a few years.

Hey, I'm all for making positive changes, but she probably should have just bought something used in her price range.

"There's no accounting for taste."

...but I kind of wish there was.

Wouldn't it be great to get a year-end statement on your tongue?

FOR THE FISCAL YEAR 2012

ACCOUNTING FOR BRYAN ALLAIN'S TASTE

Total savory foods consumed – 1040

Total sweet foods consumed – 688

Total times gross items were tasted upon an "Ugh, you've got to try this." request – 5

Total number of taste buds burnt by impatient coffee drinking - 27

Total number of bags of Tostitos Hint of Lime chips consumed - 71

Percentage of those chips consumed after 9pm - 97%

Total number of bull testicles consumed - 0 (36th year in a row!)

Total times ear wax was tasted from a pen that was previously inserted into ear – 4

"She did it on a shoestring budget."

...and frankly we shouldn't have been surprised.

Anyone with the patience to write our their entire budget on a shoelace is more than capable of successfully managing a few thousand dollars.

YOU ARE WHAT YOU EAT

"He's going to eat us out of house and Home!"

I get the 'Eat us out of house' part. If you were living with someone who literally ate everything in sight, the cost of the food would force you to miss mortgage payments and eventually lose your house to the bank.

But the home, too?

Can someone eat so much that it breaks up the very bonds of the family unit?

Can the fibers of love that hold our families together be shredded to bits by an insatiable hunger?

Can a greedy stomach destroy the unconditional love between a mother and her suckling babe?

I don't know, and I don't want to know. Pass me that bag of Hint of Lime chips.

"Yeah, but that's like comparing apples to oranges."

Why is it wrong to compare apples and oranges? They're both pieces of fruit...what's the big deal?

Apples are less messy to eat and offer a wider variety of choices. Oranges taste better and make a better juice.

You see, I just compared them, and I like oranges better. Was that really that hard?

The next time you hear "that's like comparing apples and oranges" interject with a comparison that's actually difficult. Here are a few suggestions:

It's like comparing apples and scissors.

It's like comparing wristbands and ear wax.

It's like comparing Rod Stewart and microwave ovens.

It's like comparing blocked bowels and the DHARMA Initiative.

It's like comparing anxiety attacks and Roger Federer's toothbrush.

It's like comparing ampersands and mime costumes.

I think you get the point.

May we never go apples and oranges ever again.

"That guy is really worth his salt."

I'm gonna need you to clarify this one for me.

Is he worth his WEIGHT in salt? Because that dude goes about 225-230. Last time I checked that much salt will cost you over $500, even if you buy it in bulk.

Unless you're saying that he's only worth the amount of salt in his body, which at only seven tablespoons (thanks Wikipedia!) will set you back a few bucks. Kind of insulting, to be honest.

Or maybe he's the kind of dude who carries around salt packets in his pocket just in case he stumbles into some unsalted french fries? Or maybe he likes salt on a watermelon. Have you met these salt on a watermelon people? They're insane. Except for my mom, who just read a draft of this book and apparently also likes salt on a watermelon. She's an angel.

Point is, the only way this expression isn't a huge insult is if the guy your talking about owns a salt mine or the property deed for the Dead Sea. Otherwise, let's hope the guy is worth a lot more than just his salt.

"It's as easy as pie."

Is it as easy as baking a pie or as easy as eating a pie?

Baking a pie isn't very easy from what I've heard. You've got to prepare the crust, deal with the filling, cook it for just the right amount of time, and pray that cartoon birds don't eat it while it's cooling on your windowsill.

But eating a pie?

Easier than breathing (and arguably more important).

"Don't cry over spilled milk."

Seriously, if you're going to cry, go do it somewhere else.

When the leucine enkephalin in your tears mixes with the phospholipids in the milk it makes it a real bear to get out of the carpets.

Go cry into the toilet or over the plants in the family room, you baby.

"Everything from soup to nuts."

What spectrum could we possibly be talking about in which soup is all the way on one side and nuts are all the way over on the other side?

The Spectrum of Idiotic Food Clichés?

I spent an entire day trying to make sense of this one and the best I can figure is that the world's first grocery store had canned soup in the first aisle and the nuts in the last.

"Sweep the entire store, stock boy, and don't skip any aisles. Clean it all, everything from soup to nuts!"

If only they sold cans of "hours of your life back" in that supermarket so I could buy 24 of them and we could call it even.

"Hot enough to fry an egg on the sidewalk."

But is it hot enough to enjoy an entire breakfast?

For that you'd need it to be...

...so hot that you can also toast bread on a sewer grate.

...so hot that you can brew filtered coffee using a hose and a gym sock.

...so hot that if you need cheese for your omelet, you can squeeze it right out of the cow's udders.

...so hot that you'd even consider eating an unfrosted pop-tart. (Eating one of those freaking things is like eating a trade paperback.)

...so hot that Aunt Jemima is wearing a bathing suit in public for the first time in 23 years.

...so hot that if you even think about touching my Eggo, I will punch you in the larynx.

...so hot that Tony the Tiger and the Trix Rabbit are sucking on the same ice cube.

...so hot that the Lucky Charms guy is grilling up Toucan Sam on the driveway.

...so hot that, well, you get the picture.

"He's the bread winner of the family."

But the truth is they'd be able to afford some meat and potatoes to go with that bread if he was gainfully employed.

Heck, he doesn't even need to get a job; he just needs to enter contests that offer a better first prize than bread.

"The proof is in the pudding."

...and suddenly this has turned into the greatest day ever in the life on this CSI agent.

Last week the proof was in puddle of blood. The week before that, it was at the bottom of shallow grave filled with unleaded gasoline and Philip Seymour Hoffman's toenail clippings.

And don't even get me started on the septic tank debacle of '96.

But mmm...pudding.

"That's the way the cookie crumbles."

Actually, that's the way everything crumbles.

Big pieces become smaller pieces which break down to itty-bitty bits of cookie that you hate to waste so you lick your thumb and press it into the dust when no one's looking and stick your thumb into your mouth, only your wife is not amused because she saw you, as did the Thompsons, and now you're going to argue for 45 minutes about manners and politeness when they leave instead of making out to the new Norah Jones album as you had been planning to do since you bought it this morning.

Oh well, that's the way the cookie crumbles.

"She's rolling in the dough."

And if anyone from the Food and Drug Administration catches her doing it, her bakery will be shut down immediately, and she'll go back to being broke in her parent's basement with nothing but a couple of rolling pins and her creepy yeast fetish.

"You won't amount to a hill of beans."

Have you ever seen a hill of beans? Me either. But I'll be honest, chances are I would be extremely impressed.

"You mean this hill I'm looking at...this entire mound...is made out of beans? Wow. That's amazing. I mean, I can't imagine how many beans are in there and how long it must have taken to pile them up like that. It's really something to behold. I'm impressed. I'm just...really impressed."

So you know what, you're right. Maybe I won't amount to a hill of beans. Maybe people won't be amazed and astonished every time they see me. But that's okay.

Trying to amount to a hill of beans was setting the bar way too high.

I'm shooting for a mound of rice.

"That's not really my cup of tea."

I know it's not your cup of tea.

It's not anyone's cup of tea because it's not a cup, and it has nothing to do with brewed tea leaves.

It's an activity I do with random strangers I meet online, and so I'll ask you again, "Do you want to come coed, naked, outdoor figure skating with me this afternoon or not?"

"Don't bite the hand that feeds you."

Especially if you're by yourself sitting on the couch eating Doritos.

"He's really got egg on his face now."

And he SHOULD be extremely embarrassed.

Not because he did that thing that let everyone know how irresponsible he is, but because he eats breakfast like an 18-month old. There's yolk all over his chin and a piece of egg white dangling from his right nostril.

Learn how to use a napkin, chick-murderer.

"He's got champagne tastes and a beer budget."

And it's what ultimately caused Jon and Sharon to default on their mortgage.

Whenever she questioned how he could come home with six new bottles of champagne every day, he would just tell her the state of their budget for alcohol, which somehow was never overdrawn.

What she didn't know was that their "alcohol" budget was strictly for beer. The champagne was coming out of the "Miscellaneous" fund, which he overdrew by about $1800 every month because of his questionable budgeting practices and his insatiable predilection for the bubbly stuff.

Somewhere, Dave Ramsey is shaking his head in total disgust.

"One foot on a banana peel and the other in the grave."

Was it kind of creepy for him to be stepping into an open burial plot at the local cemetery after eating a banana?

Absolutely.

But still creepier was the fact that one of his legs was over six feet long.

Mutant.

"She acted like a kid in a candy store!"

So you're saying she was indecisive and whiny because she couldn't get everything she wanted to the point where you had to tell her, "Look, I don't need to buy you anything here. I thought it would be nice to treat you to one thing, but if you're going to have this attitude we're not getting anything, and you'll be grounded from the Wii and the computer for the rest of the weekend; do you understand?"

Got it.

Actually, Clams Are Miserable

AQUARIUMS TO ZOOS

"Let's not open up that can of worms."

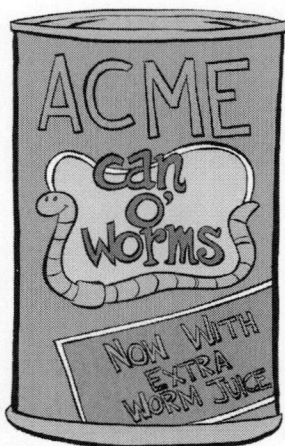

If I asked you to go buy me an unopened can of worms, how long would it take you?

A day? A week? Longer than it took for James Cameron to make *Avatar*?

From now on, the only people who are allowed to use this expression are people who have actually seen an unopened can of worms.

(And like Keyser Soze, that expression is *poof* gone.)

"I felt like a fish out of water."

Oh, wow. I'm sorry to hear that you felt like you were 90 seconds away from dying.

What's that? You weren't about to die, you were just trying to say that you were slightly uncomfortable?

Hm…

So when a fish is flopping around on the bottom of the boat, gasping for just one more sip of life-giving water, you would call that situation "slightly uncomfortable"?

You have no soul.

"He just quit, cold turkey."

Can we get a scientist on line 1 to explain what happens to turkey meat when it is refrigerated? What phenomenon is occurring on the molecular level that gives it the properties of an immediate quitter when it drops below 40 degrees Fahrenheit?

Maybe with that human genome project wrapping up we can we get our brightest minds on this bad boy.

And while we're here, if quitting something "cold turkey" means quitting it completely and immediately, the next time someone you know needs to drop a bad habit tell them, "You better throw that turkey in the fridge, sucka!"

"The early bird gets the worm."

Yeah, but the late bird gets to sleep in. And as long as it rained the night before, there will be enough worms for everyone to eat like kings.

You should see my driveway the morning after a hard rain. It's worm genocide.

"She's as happy as a clam."

Are you sure you want to use a clam as the standard for happiness?

Not only are bivalve mollusks incapable of feeling emotions, but even if they could, they have no face to show it.

And if we suspend our disbelief to assume that they could feel happiness and had a face to show it, what exactly do you suppose they would be happy about?

They spend their entire lives burrowed in sediment until one day they're plucked from their home by the Gorton's fisherman only to end up in your $2.99 cup of chowder at Panera Bread.

Some life.

"It's about ten miles as the crow flies."

If it's ten miles to your house 'as the crow flies', what you're saying is if I travel towards your house, then poop in a tree for a few minutes, then circle my neighbor's backyard long enough to creep them out, then find my way over to the roof of the mall and hang out with my buddies, then shamelessly eat possum guts on a backroad, THEN arrive at your house, I will have traveled about ten miles?

I think I'll just stick to paved roads and see you in two minutes.

"A bird in the hand is worth two in the bush."

I'd like to poke holes in this statement, but in the end, it makes complete logical sense.

Do you know how much having two birds in a bush is worth to me?

Answer: nothing.

Do you know how much having a bird in my hand is worth to me?

Answer: nothing.

So the statement is technically true. A bird in the hand IS worth two in the bush.

Thank you, mathematics!

"There's more than one way to skin a cat."

Nope, pretty sure there's just one.

Take a sharp blade, and peel off the skin.

That's it. That's the list.

"She was as drunk as a skunk."

So what you're saying is, "She's completely sober," since skunks are incapable of opening a bottle of beer or pouring themselves a shot of Jameson.

And why a skunk? Is it just because it rhymes? If that's the only reason, let me suggest a few possible improvements:

"She's as drunk as a monk."

Granted, most monks don't binge drink, but unlike skunks, they do have opposable thumbs and refrigerators to store Guinness.

"She's as drunk as a punk."

Rebellious high schoolers are into all sorts of crap these days. Plus, when you weigh 75 pounds, all it takes is a half of a Coors Light to get you tipsy.

"She's as drunk as Theodore the Chipmunk."

If you insist on going with an animal, at least pick one that lives like a human, has a beer belly, and has a reason to drink. (No way I could live with that Dave guy. What a whiner.)

"It's raining cats and dogs out there."

I've got a bachelor's degree, a clear head, and a full stomach, and I still can't make any sense out of this train wreck of an expression. Ever say this around children? Their puzzled expressions say it all.

Look, if you insist on using animals to describe how hard it's raining, at the very least mix it up a little. Here are my top five replacement ideas:

5. It's raining rats and anteaters out there! (I feel like we need to utilize the anteater more in everyday life.)

4. It's raining penguins and polar bears out there! (For a cold, November rain*.)

3. It's raining ticks and gnats out there! (Use this for a light, misty rain, obviously.)

2. It's raining tigers and pandas out there! (Using endangered species is a way to describe rainfall during a drought. I know, I know, it's brilliant.)

and my personal favorite...

1. It's raining free range bison and peregrine falcons out there!

* *nothing lasts forever*

"What, were you raised by wolves?"

The next time someone asks you this because you're not eating as politely as they'd like or because your room is messy, say, "Yes, actually I was raised by wolves."

Then, roll around on the ground to mark your scent, howl at them for a few minutes, and rip them limb from limb with your teeth.

Who's the jokester now, mangled carcass?

"Well I'll be a monkey's uncle!"

So, not only are you demanding that one of your brothers or sisters marry a monkey, but you're also putting immediate pressure on them to have a kid?

You might make a great uncle someday, but you're a lousy sibling.

"I'll be there in two shakes of a lamb's tail."

Having very limited exposure to the hindquarters of a sheep, I'm not sure what to make of this one.

I imagine a lamb's tail shakes very fast by itself, which if that's true means you'll be here in about 1.5 seconds. Fantastic! Thanks for being so prompt.

Unless, of course, a lamb's tail doesn't move by itself at all. Maybe it just hangs there, and you have to physically shake it with your hand. If that's the case, I'm guessing you're not going to be here for a while.

Sure, you might be able to sneak up on it and get that first shake right away.

But once he's wise to your game? That second shake could take hours.

LET ME HEAR YOUR BODY TALK

"He was born with a silver spoon in his mouth."

...and it's a good thing his parents are rich enough to afford the reconstructive surgery.

That spoon did some serious damage to mom's birthing canal on the way out.

"From the mouths of babes."

How this expression ever garnered a positive connotation is beyond me.

For every cute 'googoo' and 'gaga' that comes out of a baby's mouth, you get 41 spit-ups, 117 screaming fits, and 50 "my diaper is a hot mess" wails.

It makes me wonder if the expression used to be longer and it was mistakenly truncated at some point.

Don't these versions of it make way more sense:

"From the mouths of babes comes anguish and chaos."

"From the mouths of babes come vile fluids that warrant keeping an open tab at the dry cleaners."

"From the mouths of babes come 3:30am wake up calls that could kill a rooster."

Don't get me wrong, I love babies. I'm just not a big fan of their mouths.

"He has his nose to the grindstone."

Such a gruesome, painful way to say you're gonna work hard.

Although with a nose like mine, losing an inch or two off the ole schnoz might not be a bad idea.

"He has ice water in his veins."

Ice water is great, but you know what will really make you clutch under pressure? Having 98.6 degree blood in your veins.

I guarantee you'll be much more capable of hitting the game winning shot when your hypothermia-induced corpse isn't sprawled out on the free throw line.

"I'm hoping I can rub elbows with someone important."

When applied literally, this is one of the worst things you could possibly do at a party or social gathering. Networking should never involve getting to second base with the back of someone's arm.

And if we're going to refer to rubbing body parts with someone as successful networking, why the elbow? It's so dry and bony. How about "rubbing palms" or "rubbing calves"?

"You going to that party on Tuesday night?"

"Yeah, I'm hoping I can rub midriffs with a few of the bigwigs from the company."

"Best of luck!"

"She's busier than a one-armed paper hanger."

Forget her, let's talk about the paper hanger and his choice of professions.

That dude needs a career counselor and a Monster.com account, like, yesterday.

"I really need to get this off my chest."

You're right buddy; you do need to get it off your chest.

But honestly, you should have just told me your secret instead of writing it all over your man-boobs in permanent marker.

Good luck scrubbing that off without rubbing your nipples raw.

"It's all fun and games until someone loses an eye."

...at which point it's still games; it's just not much fun anymore.

I mean, I'm not gonna lie. I'm pretty good at "Who Can Grab the Rolling Eyeball While it's Owner Flails On the Ground in Searing Pain," but I wouldn't call it 'fun'.

"He's a real breath of fresh air."

So he's like a U.F.O., right?

Because I don't care how many Altoids you shove in your mouth, there's nothing fresh about a human's warm, moist breath.

If you're claiming this guy really is a breath of fresh air, you must be trying to say that he doesn't exist.

Oh look, there he goes now riding off into that triple rainbow sunset with Bigfoot on twin unicorns! I take it all back!

"You really put your foot in your mouth that time."

What you said was so dumb, the only way for anyone to forget about it is for you to take off your shoe and sock and stick your bare foot into your own mouth, leaving us all confused and slightly nauseous.

Actually, now that you've done it, I think we all realize that was a mistake, too.

You will forever be known as the flexible guy with weird toes who says stupid things.

"I'm keeping my eye on you."

...and I'm pretty confident that as long as my squishy, wet eyeball is touching your stomach you'll be too grossed out to do anything stupid.

"He's a little long in the tooth."

Wait, how long has he been in the tooth? I've lost count at this point, but what a nightmare.

When Phil was magically shrunken to the size of a Tic-Tac, I thought he had seen the worst of it. But then his nemesis had him placed into a fake incisor in his mouth, where's Phil's been trapped ever since. Think of all the bad breath he's experienced. All the biting, the burping, the grinding, the vomit, and that disgusting habit he has of chewing wheat thins into a mushy paste and then putting two new wheat thins into his mouth to make a mushy paste sandwich.

That's a long time to be in the tooth.

"I'm all ears."

...and I'm the most disgusting human being on the face of the earth because my entire body is made out of ears.

I know I'm ghastly, but must you scream so loudly? I have very sensitive hearing.

Oh, and sorry about all the wax.

"I made it by the skin of my teeth."

No, seriously I just barely made it, and look, I barely have skin on my teeth, so the expression works.

What's that? Why do I have skin on my teeth?

Oh, because I'm a cannibal. I eat skin. And meat. From humans.

Again, I apologize for barging in here last minute with such poor hygiene. I would have flossed, but I knew that would have made me late.

By the way, has anyone ever told you that you have great skin tone and a remarkable complexion? Come a little closer so I can get a better look.

"We're seeing eye to eye on this."

And while it's nice to be in agreement with you, the view really sucks.

Your iris is really starting to freak me out. And every time you blink it tickles my retina in a way that makes me want to soak my clothes in kerosene and throw myself into a raging bonfire.

Are we seeing eye to eye on that, too?

"Why don't you put your money where your mouth is."

So you'd like me to remove everything in my checking account and staple it between my nose and chin?

Not sure how that's going to help my case, but if that's what it will take for you to believe me, I'll do it.

"He really rubs me the wrong way."

...and come to think of it, there is no right way.

FIRE, WATER, & OTHER WEAPONS

"Don't throw the baby out with the bath water."

Let's get one thing straight from the start: no one in the history of the world has ever purposefully or accidentally thrown out the baby with the bath water.

No matter how nasty or disgusting the bath water is, I can guarantee no parent has ever considered ditching the baby because of it. *"Ew, this water is slightly discolored...jettison this child!"*

Let's not also forget that here in the 21st century most of us don't throw out bath water anymore thanks to the invention of the drain.

So put down your pail, close the window, and go cuddle with that toddler you were about to heave. And let's never speak of this again.

"You need to just bite the bullet."

Legend has it this expression originated when they gave wounded soldiers a bullet to bite on during surgical procedures before the invention of anesthesia.

Maybe I'm an idiot, but couldn't we have found something less dangerous for these guys to stick between their clenched teeth than a live round? A rock, perhaps? A piece of wood? An rabid mongoose with multiple open wounds?

As if having a limb amputated without meds wasn't bad enough, why not take the chance of having all of your teeth blown out of your mouth as well?

"Maybe we can kill two birds with one stone."

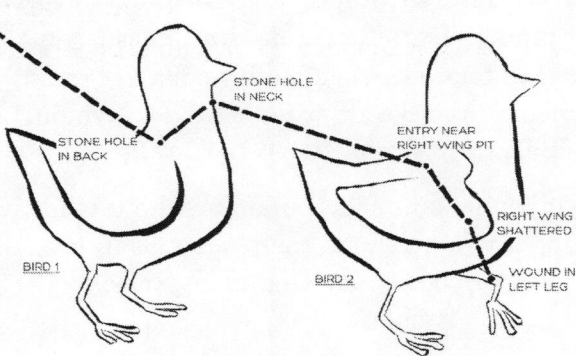

ALLAIN'S MAGIC STONE THEORY
STONE FROM
ASSASSIN'S HAND
60' HIGH

STONE HOLE
IN NECK

STONE HOLE
IN BACK

ENTRY NEAR
RIGHT WING PIT

RIGHT WING
SHATTERED

BIRD 1

BIRD 2

WOUND IN
LEFT LEG

Have you ever tried to kill ONE bird with one stone? Not easy, my friend.

Going for a two for one is like trying to win the lottery twice in one week playing the same numbers.

This expression should really mean, "let's do something needlessly violent and completely impossible."

"He who lives by the sword, dies by the sword."

That's because most people die in their houses, the same place where most sword owners keep their sword.

So if you have a sword stashed somewhere in your house, of course you are going to die by it. It's common sense, really.

"That's as useless as a screen door on a submarine."

This expression makes perfect sense until you stop and think about it.

What would you rather drown in?

A) a submarine filled with ocean water, sharks, electric eels, sea urchins, and dolphin poop.

B) a submarine filled with filtered ocean water and nothing else.

C) a vat of boiling vinegar

Hm.

Maybe that screen door isn't so useless after all.

"When it rains, it pours."

I refuse to agree with such a ridiculous, generalizing statement and in doing so spit upon the good names of misting and drizzling.

Also a fun exercise: carry this expression into other areas of life.

...when it snows, it blizzards.

...when he naps, he hibernates.

...when it breaks, it disintegrates.

...when she works, she works late nights and weekends and eventually burns out which leads to her getting a tattoo of an eagle on her neck because she was drowning her sorrows in liquor and she never turns down a dare when she's drunk, even if it's a random stranger at a bar daring her to get a bird of prey tattooed above her collarbone.

...when he cries, he ugly cries.

...when she craps, she explosive diarrheas.

Let's move on.

"Cry me a river."

Forget a river. I'm not convinced your body is capable of producing enough water to create a stream. I mean, even if your entire body mass turned to water, you'd be nothing more than a small puddle that a few sheets of Bounty could soak up.

How about this? If you can somehow produce enough tears to form even a mini tributary, I'll apologize for whatever it was I did.

"She's as right as rain."

If I had to list five hundred adjectives I might use to describe rain, the word "right" wouldn't even sniff the list. When would rain ever be right?

After weeks of meditation and soul searching I can only come up with three scenarios:

1) You're a farmer, and your crops are about to dry up and die; and if it doesn't rain in the next day or two, you're going to have to sell the farm and go back to contract killing.

2) You're a kid who signed up to play baseball, and now you hate it, but your parents won't let you quit, so you have to go to practice twice a week, except for when it rains and practice is canceled and you can just sit at home and play XBox instead.

3) You're a former farmer, and a current contract killer, and you need to bury a body in your backyard, but the ground is frozen, and what you really need is a good soaking rain to loosen up the earth so you can hide your latest "carcass harvest".

Other than those scenarios, rain isn't right; it's just wet.

"I'm feeling a little under the weather."

If people only said this when they were feeling sick on miserable, rainy days, I'd be ok with it. The problem is, they say it no matter what the weather.

NEW RULE: you can only use this expression if your mood matches the weather.

So if it's a beautiful day and you feel great, you're feeling "under the weather".

If it's cold and rainy and you feel like you were just run over by a hearse, you're feeling "under the weather".

If you are in the peaceful eye of a hurricane and you just enjoyed a relaxing massage despite the fact that you got fired yesterday and you're going to jail tomorrow for tax evasion and three counts of impersonating a federal judge while dealing narcotics, you're "feeling under the weather".

Done and done.

"I'll be a son of a gun."

To be honest, I didn't have much of a choice.

My daddy really did love that female rifle of his.*

---

*neither the author, nor the publisher, condones romantic relationships between humans and firearms. If you or someone you love is intimately involved with a firearm, please seek help immediately with a local, accredited counselor. And please, for the love of all things good and true, never cuddle with your gun without the safety on.

"He has too many irons in the fire."

Hearing this cliché makes me want to jump into Doc Brown's time machine and interview a blacksmith from the 1800s. Was having too many irons in the fire that big of an issue that it spawned its own expression?

Seems to me having too many irons in the fire would mean that business was booming. Wouldn't that be a good thing? I mean, the irons are just sitting there in the fire staying really hot. It's not like the blacksmith was juggling them all blindfolded.

Now, if you had too many hot irons lying on a pile of dry kindling, I could see how that would be an issue.

Too many irons in your bed? Yeah, that's probably not gonna work out if you want eight hours of sleep.

And sure, having too many irons laying on the chest of your 91-year old grandfather would likely be a problem as well. The weight would eventually crush his fragile sternum and lungs.

But too many irons in the fire?

Seems like a non-issue to me.

"Don't pee on my leg and tell me it's raining."

You had me at leg.

"Why don't we just bury the hatchet?"

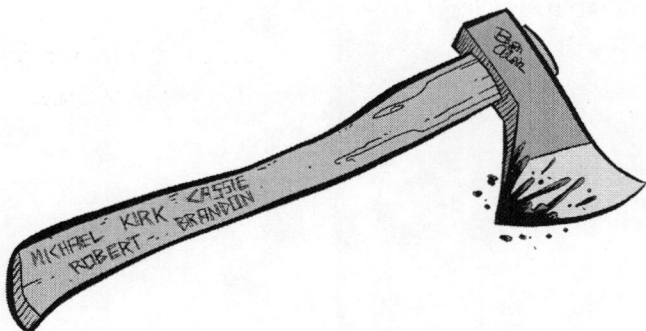

...and let's hope no one around here owns a metal detector, because if they dig that thing up, our fingerprints are all over it. And blood. There's a lot of blood on that hatchet.

Now that I think of it, carving the names of our victims into the wooden handle was probably a bit much. So was autographing the blade in a sharpie. Maybe we shouldn't have argued about that for so long.

You know what? Less talking, more digging.

"Don't shoot the messenger!"

...and for future reference, even if I'm not the messenger next time, don't shoot me then either.

In fact, here's a new rule of thumb for all our future interactions: no matter what I am, never shoot me.

"You brought a knife to a gun fight."

Three things need to be addressed here:

1. I personally don't have to worry about this one because I don't own a fighting knife. I own butter knives and serrated steak knives, but I'd sooner show up to a fight with a foam trident than one of those.

2. If I catch wind of a gun fight happening nearby, pretty safe bet I'm not gonna show up to it. In fact, there are three places in this world where I can guarantee you will never find me: A gun fight, an air show, and Nickelback's green room.

3. Are we sure that gunfights ever happened in the Old West? Were people really that angry and dumb that they thought the best way to settle their differences was for the slowest gun shooter to die? Seems like the second dumbest way to settle an argument in the history of the world. (Number One, of course, is appearing on *Judge Judy*.)

"Where there's smoke, there's fire."

Or a fog machine.

Or smoldering embers from a youth group campfire.

Or a kid burning a leaf with a magnifying glass before burning an ant with a magnifying glass and then feeling kind of bad about it.

Or a stick of patchouli incense.

Or a bunch of seventh graders with marlboro lights trying to find their identity.

Or a monster on LOST.

Or coughing. Where there's smoke, there's always coughing.

AROUND THE HOUSE

"Someone got up on the wrong side of the bed."

What gave it away?

Was it the scowl on his face, the cobwebs in his hair, or the bruise on his forehead from slamming into the underside of the box spring?

Maybe when he calmed down he'd be able to figure out how he ended up sleeping under his bed in the first place. Until then, you might want to stay clear.

"Don't judge someone until you've walked a mile in their shoes."

Recognizing this legal loophole, Nancy wore the tallest stilettos she had to court on the first day of her trial.

She knew there was no way the portly Judge Wilson would be able to make it around the block four times in her size six heels, and as such, a mistrial would have to be granted.

"He's as cute as a button."

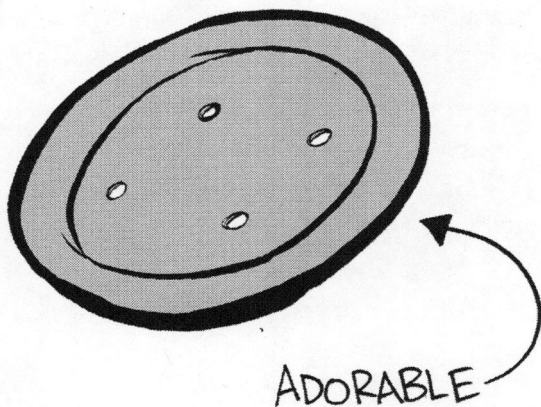

ADORABLE

There is nothing, and I mean nothing, even remotely cute about a button.

If you really think about it, this should be a cruel insult.

'Oh, look at him! He's as cute as a small plastic disc with four symmetrical holes.'

Snaps aren't handsome, zippers aren't sexy, and buttons are definitely not cute.

"It's as clear as a bell."

So in other words, it's not clear at all.

Every bell I've ever seen in my entire life was made out of an opaque metal.

"It was nothing to write home about."

Since the invention of the telephone, this expression now applies to everything in the entire world.

"It's as clean as a whistle."

There are few things in this world as UNCLEAN as a whistle, which in case you've forgotten is a small piece of metal or plastic that spends 95% of its life in an old referee's hand, pocket, and mouth.

I can think of 10 disgusting things off the top of my head that I'd rather put in my own mouth than a whistle:

1. a used stick of deodorant

2. the spit valve of a third grader's trumpet

3. a dead bird

4. the pine tar rag from the visiting on deck circle at Wrigley Field

5. a Rosie O'Donnell burp

6. a soiled band-aid

7. lava

8. Keith Richards' sweatiest guitar pick

9. acid rain collected in a rotting tortoise shell

10. the bathroom doorknob at a Burger King

Shouldn't we be saying, 'dirty as a whistle'?

"You make a better door than a window."

I get it. You can't see the TV when I'm standing in front of you. You are so clever.

But would I really make a better door? Could you hinge my body to a door frame and use me to keep people out of your living room? Can you install a latch and a lock in my right palm? Are you skilled enough to construct a door frame the exact size of my body to prevent drafts and bugs from getting in? And if so, wouldn't it be really awkward trying to step through a door frame that was the shape of my silhouette?

I think a better expression would have been "You make a better wall than a window," or "You make a better vessel for housing organs and a soul than a window," or "please get out of the way".

"Stop beating around the bush!"

Few people know this, but this saying originated from a marital spat.

Wife: "Hey, come out here and help me get this stray cat out of our hedges."

Husband: "Dang cats are always getting in our stuff. I've had enough."

Wife: "Well, I can't get the thing to leave. I keep whacking the ground with this shovel, but it won't move."

Husband: "Well, stop beating around the bush."

Wife: "What do you propose I should do?"

Husband: "I don't know, just beat the dang bush. Swing the shovel at the bush and hope it hits the cat. Or get the chainsaw out and cut the bush down. Or use the shovel to dig a moat around the bush, fill the moat with kerosene, and call down fire like Elijah. I don't care what you do so long as you stop beating around the freaking bush; it ain't doing any good."

True story. Now you know.

"You made your bed; now you have to lie in it."

I've always been baffled by this one. When it's time to sleep, I could care less what condition the bed is in.

Granted, if the bed is made then it's going to take a little extra effort to get the covers pulled back so I can get comfortable, but is it so much of an issue that we need to build an expression around it?

But hey, I could be wrong. Maybe this is a problem for some people?

If you're the type of person who gets ready for bed, realizes that you made your bed earlier in the day, and is so discouraged that you decide to sleep on the couch, let us know so we can all make fun of you until you cry.

"We need to push the envelope."

I've read an envelope, tossed an envelope, taped an envelope, licked an envelope, burnt an envelope, filed an envelope, bought an envelope, stolen an envelope, kissed an envelope (don't ask, it was a dark period), crumpled an envelope, ripped an envelope, lost an envelope, found an envelope, stuffed an envelope, shredded an envelope, and farted in an envelope.

But I can't say I've ever pushed one.

Actually, Clams Are Miserable

BYGONES AND HAYSTACKS

"I'll make you cry uncle."

...because the first thing I think of when I'm in a lot of pain and want someone to stop hurting me is my father's brother.

"Rome wasn't built in a day."

Yeah, no crap. Nobody ever said it was.

You can't build anything in a day.

It takes me three days to put together a lego police boat for my son; you think I'm under the impression that an entire city was built in 24 hours?

"Great minds think alike."

Every technological advance we have is due to the fact that people think differently. Otherwise, you'd be reading this book via smoke signal or telegram. Stop. And that would be annoying. Stop. You see what I mean? Stop.

Have you ever noticed that this expression is never uttered when it's two genuinely great minds involved? It's either one bright guy and one idiot, in which case the bright guy smiles and thinks to himself "how dare you?" or it's two dolts trying to make each other feel good after discussing the worst idea of all time.

(And if you agreed with all that, smile and say to yourself 'great minds think alike.')

"He marches to the beat of a different drummer."

Wait, is the beat different, or is the drummer different?

I mean, if it's a different drummer, is that really a big deal? Ask any drummer to lay down something you can march to, and they'll be all over it.

But marching to a different beat? That could get interesting.

Ever seen anyone try to march to a 5/4 time signature?

It's a hot mess.

"You're just grasping at straws."

Have you ever grasped for straws? It's really not as hard as they make it out to be.

Straws typically come in 100-count boxes, and all you do is reach in and grab one.

Does it get tricky if your kid wants a blue one and you keep grasping pink and green? Sure. But with a little persistence and a functioning opposable thumb, it really isn't hard.

I feel like the people who turned this into a cliché were really grasping at straws.

"Let's let bygones be bygones."

I never wanted bygones to be anything other than bygones, so I've got no problem with that.

"Let's not reinvent the wheel here."

Why are we all so worried about reinventing the wheel?

Are we really that happy with the wheel we have?

I know it works great and all, but what if there's something better out there? Some shape we haven't thought of yet that's more efficient?

Someday when the wheel is rendered obsolete by an MIT undergrad, we're all going to feel like idiots for saying, "I don't want to reinvent the wheel" so often.

Don't say I didn't warn you.

"It's like looking for a needle in a haystack."

You're trying to tell me that this is an impossible situation, but that's not what I'm hearing at all.

When you say, "it's like looking for a needle in a haystack," I'm thinking one of three things:

1) "This situation is easy as long as I have the right tools." (Give me a metal detector, and I'll find your needle in about five minutes.)

2) "This situation is dumb." (Needles cost how much, four cents each? Go buy a new one.)

3) "This situation is your own fault" (Who sews on a stack of hay, anyway? Ever heard of using a chair inside of a house like a normal person?)

"It's a touch and go situation."

Is it really?

Because where I'm from, they call that sexual assault.

"When push comes to shove..."

It's like a cute little story that you forgot to finish.

"One day when Push came to Shove's house, they had a big fight because neither of them wanted to be the one who sat on the swing. The End."

When you think about it, is there really that big of a distinction between pushing and shoving?

I'd argue the words are not only interchangeable, they're combinable. And if you don't agree I will pushove you off of a cliff.

"It just vanished into thin air."

The word 'thin' must have had a great agent to get placement in this expression.

I mean, other than this cliché and any sporting event played in Denver, when was the last time you described air as thin?

Vanishing into the air is impressive enough; does it really matter if it's thin or not?

"It's time to face the music."

Is it really though? Because the cool thing about music is your ear can pick up the mechanical sound waves no matter which way you're facing.

If it's okay with you, I'm going to keep facing AWAY from the music.

And while we're here, you might want to talk to the band about wearing pants for their next gig.

"I need to draw a line in the sand on this one."

So what you're saying is, you'd like us to take a stand on this now but completely abandon the position in five minutes when a wave washes it away or some punk 3-year old comes by with his shovel of mass destruction?

Got it.

"Do it like it's going out of style."

Huh?

This expression is used to imply you're doing an excessive amount of something, yet that hasn't been my experience at all when I find out something is on its way out of style.

Last Tuesday, when I found out carpenter jeans were going out of style, I certainly didn't up their usage. (I cut back to three times a week and started working in more pleated corduroys like any normal person would.)

Let's use this expression like it's not going out of style.

"It's all over but the shouting."

And since this book is done, let's get to the shouting.

THE SHOUTING

SPECIAL THANKS...

Erica - being married to you is like winning the lottery every day, only without having people hitting me up for "a few thou to start a business". Thanks for always laughing at me (and with me). You are the best ever.

Kylie and Parker - you're two of the funniest kids I know and I'm so proud to be your dad. Keep laughing at life and at yourself. Love you both so much.

My blog readers - Without you this book would be nothing more than a few scattered ideas bouncing around in my brain. Thanks for reading!

Mom and Dad - thanks for helping me get through that very extended bedwetting season. Love you for that and for the countless other things you've done for me.

Josh, Karyn, Steph, and Jordan - someday maybe I'll write a book telling ridiculous stories from growing up together. Seven people, one bathroom, and lots of "I have to poop" dances in the hallway. Love you guys!

Tyler Stanton - thanks for punching up a few of these jokes for me. Looking forward to returning the favor on your television show someday.

John Marenovich - You are a made up person that is an inside joke in our family. Thank you for always being there for us when we need a punchline.

REGULAR THANKS...

My funny friends - I thought of you as I wrote this book, trying to make each joke the best it could be so I could make you snicker. Thanks for being so funny and good-looking.

My unfunny friends - I didn't think of you as I wrote this book because I didn't want your crappy senses of humor influencing me. But thanks for being good friends nonetheless, and for being so good-looking.

Everyone else - Thanks for not murdering me up to this point in my life. It played a huge role in helping me finish this book. I couldn't have done it without you not murdering me, so thanks!

ABOUT THE AUTHOR

Bryan Allain is a humor writer, blog coach, and mammal who lives in Lancaster County, PA with his wife Erica and their two kids, Kylie and Parker.

You can find him online at KillerTribes.com helping people find their fans and extend their reach through resources, events, and an online community. He also writes a few times a week at BryanAllain.com, a website named after an American hero. He is not Amish.

Made in the USA
Charleston, SC
11 November 2012